Jeffrey Grenfell-Hill trained for the professional theatre at the Bristol Old Vic Theatre School, where he was chosen to be student director in the final year. After a tour of American colleges, universities and performing arts centres, he was invited to join the examining board of the London Academy of Music and Dramatic Art.

His poems have appeared in Penguin and Heinemann anthologies. Samuel French have published his plays, and his monologues for young actors have been published by Oberon Books in an anthology edited by Shaun McKenna. His monologues and duologues have been chosen for the LAMDA examination syllabus for the acting exams as 'set-pieces'. They are often performed as 'own choice' selections at major festivals of Speech and Drama. Jeffrey himself is an adjudicator of many years' standing with a doctorate from the University of Wales. He was Director of Sixth Form Studies at St George's School, Harpenden, where he taught A/S and A level Theatre Studies.

Jeffrey remains an examiner for the London Academy of Music and Dramatic Art and in this capacity examines both in the UK and overseas.

This book is dedicated to the memory of my aunt, Ruth Grenfell, a gifted teacher.

Jeffrey Grenfell-Hill

MONOLOGUES AND DUOLOGUES FOR YOUNG ACTORS

AUSTIN MACAULEY PUBLISHERS™

LONDON • CAMBRIDGE • NEW YORK • SHARJAH

A CIP catalogue record for this title is available from the British Library.

ISBN 9781528904544 (Paperback)
ISBN 9781528957731 (ePub e-book)

www.austinmacauley.com

First Published (2019)
Austin Macauley Publishers Ltd
25 Canada Square
Canary Wharf
London
E14 5LQ

Table of Contents

Introduction

The challenge for scriptwriters is to explore themes which the younger actor can identify with and enjoy performing. Situations that they can identify with should be the first priority. Considering this, I have created scenes set in the historical past, in a fantasy world, at school and in family situations. In all of them, one hopes that the young actor will explore emotions, deepen their understanding of various situations and heighten their awareness of dramatic possibilities.

It was Shaun McKenna, then Head of Examinations at the London Academy of Music and Dramatic Art, who edited in 1998 a most useful anthology: 'Solo Speeches for the Under 12s' (pub. by Oberon) and who sought to offer younger actors a wider choice of scenes. These proved very popular and include three of my own scenes also included in my current collection. However, it has been seventeen years since McKenna's anthology offered a wide choice to the drama teacher in junior schools and YR7 in senior schools.

Many of the scenes draw on comedic values and I believe young actors enjoy creating a sense of comedy. In the monologues, I have tried to create a sense of involvement with the unseen—with either an unseen friend or significant elements of the world around the character. The monologues ought not to be seen as a mono-thought, but a series of reactions to a multiplicity of thought patterns.

By suggesting extension work, and the building up of vocabulary, I hope to support the all-round development of the young actor. Drama should not just mean 'learning lines' but be an exploration of each situation. As a teacher myself, I want young actors to extend their vocabulary: to aim to enrich their language skills by 'becoming someone else'.

It is my intention to encourage the use of mime as a supportive element within characterisation. Some of the scenes allow for more extensive mime than others. Encourage the young actor to explore this adjunct to portrayal; it is part of the foundation blocks for insightful projection of the text.

I hope these scenes will be enjoyed by countless young actors.

Jeffrey Grenfell-Hill, Angel Cottage

Emma in 1848

The scene is a Victorian drawing room. Emma is sitting with her sister as they occupy themselves with embroidery.

EMMA: This herringbone stitch is so difficult, so very hard. But Mama says it must be done. Look, I've embroidered Noah and his ark—that was Grandmother's idea—and above it, the Lord's Prayer—which Papa suggested, and Miss Taylor made me embroider the alphabet three times in three different sizes. This has to be the biggest sampler any girl, anywhere, has ever been made to do! Mama says she will have Simpkin take it into Bath to have it framed, and it will hang in the schoolroom—the schoolroom! Really Victoria, I expected her to say the morning room at least, not the schoolroom. I shan't want to see the horrid thing ever once I've done with it.

(She throws it down.)

It must be wonderful to be a…a…dairymaid. A dairymaid would be free to do as she pleased. I'm sure they are never made to sit and embroider. Think, up with the sun, ready to milk the cows and churn the milk into butter. One could gossip, one could giggle, there'd be no such thing as 'proper behaviour', I'm sure their mothers never tell them to be more lady-like. Wishful thinking.

(She sighs and picks up the sampler again.)

When I've finished this, mama says I must embroider my initials on two-dozen handkerchiefs. Two dozen! Life is going to be an endless chain of embroidery. When I'm twelve, I'll have to start preparing my trousseau. Do you know what that means? Dozens and dozens of things. It can take years, a decade… Forever!

Things to consider as an actor:

- Try to find out what life was like for a young lady in 1848.
- What style of clothes would she be wearing? (Draw a sketch of what you might look like at this period.)
- Make a list of her feelings in this scene.
- How many moods can you find?

Vocabulary Building:
What is meant by herringbone/embroider/sampler/dairy-maid/churn/trousseau/decade?

- Remember to think of this as a scene and not just a monologue.
- Tell someone what you think of this character and why.

Notes:

The Chimney Sweep's Boy: 1852

A rather pale, scruffy boy is drinking a mug of tea at a Tea Kiosk and is telling another older boy about his life in Victorian London.

CHRIS: Orphans don't get much chance in life... Not in this city. Now see, I'm an orphan, 'bandoned I was, on the Workhus steps, at Christmas time... Cryin' my 'ed off I was... So they takes me in an'...calls me Christmas Eaves...can't say it's a name I'd choose... Not if I 'ad the choice, I'd choose like... Albert, our Queen's consort's name! It might be foreign, German like, but it's a darn sight better than Christmas! But 'pon reflection, most people call me Chris, an' that might be short for Christopher, p'raps it ain't worth bothering on.

They works you 'ard at the Workhus; when I were just three, they sends me out in the gardens stone-picking...picking up stones by the dozen... An' a right stony bit of land they built that Workhus on. Comes I'm seven an' the beagle comes an' tells the Master I got to be bound 'prentice, in the parish... An' Fred Bowles, the chimney sweep, wants a small 'un...

Now I be the smallest seven-year-old in that place. So, the Master calls me to 'im an' 'ands me over to the beagle...'an 'afore I knows what's 'appening I'm taken to Fred Bowles 'ouse 'an bound to 'im. You should 'ave seen 'is face... "Oh! I asks for a little 'un, an' I gets a midget, a veritable midget...what chimneys he shall climb... What nasty little corners he'll be able to get 'round..." 'e says all this 'as 'e dances round me, rubbin' 'is 'ands with glee.

I've been with 'im some years now, an' you can see I've not grown much. Nasty 'e is, 'specially with a nasty little fork 'e 'as which 'e prods me with when the chimney is still 'ot, an' I don't want to go any further.

"Up you goes midget," 'e says an' gives me a prod with 'is fork, it's cruel it is: "Little midgets goes all the way up." All the time, 'e is sticking those sharp tines into my backside, or my bare legs. There was two of us, another small 'un like me, called Tom, but 'e got burned alive in Lord Darnford's chimney, red 'ot it was.

But I says my prayers reg'lar like, an' hopes God is with me... An' as I climbs a really 'ot un, I says, "Please Lord, save me from dyin' an' when I gets to be a master chimney sweep, I promises never to send little boys up red 'ot chimneys." That's what I says, an' I tells you straight, I intend to keep that promise.

P'raps you can say a prayer for me too...

Things to consider as an actor:

- Try to find out what a Workhouse was?
- What does this scene tell you about Victorian London?
- What sort of life does this boy have?
- Make a list of his feelings in this scene
- How many moods can you find?

Extension work: Try to find out more about life as a chimney sweep.

Vocabulary Building: What is meant by consort/beagle/apprentice/parish/midget/veritable/prod/tines?

- Remember to think of this as a scene and not just a monologue.

- Tell someone what you think of this character and why.

The Cubs' Trip

The scene is set behind a mini-bus on which the cubs have travelled. Mick is being collected by his mother after a trip to Windsor.

MICK: Hullo, Mum! Yes, we had a great time, it was terrific… We all want to go again… Windsor Safari Park is the best place for a Cubs' outing. We all want to go again next year. Can you carry my lunch-box? I'm worn out, Mum. Really tired…

I was a bit sick on the way down, only a bit. Akela said it was because I ate my fish-paste sandwiches as soon as I got on the bus… But I was hungry… Then I had the Turkish delight bars, then a drop of Coke. Roger didn't like me being sick all over him, but I couldn't help it. It was the second can of Coke that did it… Then I was starving when we got to Windsor, so Roger gave me his cheese sandwiches which he didn't want after me being sick.

What…my shoes… What happened to my shoes? Well, I know they're a bit muddy… Yes, it is up to my ankles, but I couldn't help it… It happened when Roger got a bit scratched, only a bit… He was waving his arm about…that is, outside the mini-bus…only a little bit out, like two or three fingers…and this baboon came along and grabbed it… Well, it wouldn't let go, so I leaned out of the window, caught the door latch and it flew open and I fell down into the mud… It wasn't too muddy and I didn't mind… Well, then the baboon made a grab for me, and I got scratched too (rolls up jumper and shows arm) but at least Roger got his arm in. Then Akela tried to pull me in, but fell out… Well, he fell on top of me, but I managed to climb back in, so the baboon scratched Akela a bit… Perhaps a bit more than me…a bit… And we all want to club together to send him a 'Get Well Card'…yes! We had to leave Akela at Windsor General Hospital…

It was definitely the best Cub trip we've ever had, better than that trip we had to Clacton-On-Sea which was dead boring…

But, oh! Gosh, I'm really exhausted, Mum.

Things to consider as an actor:

- What would a Safari Park be like?
- How does Mick feel about the day in this scene?
- What is happening in this scene
- How many moods are there?

Extension work: Try to find out all you can about baboons.

Vocabulary Building:
What is meant by fish-paste/safari/Turkish delight/Akela?

- Remember to think of this as a scene and not just a monologue.
- Tell someone what you think of this character and why.

Notes:

The Brownies Pet Show

The scene is set in Sophie's home, where she is sitting at a table and cutting out shapes which she is sticking into a book.

SOPHIE: Brown Owl's bright idea this year was a Brownie Pet show... It seemed like a really good idea... We all have pets, well most of us that is, except Lucinda Dingle and she's allergic to feathers, fur, dust, milk, oranges, tomatoes AND her mother! At the moment, her mother's feeding her on goats milk and cheese 'cos she has a permanent rash all over her nose. She told Brown Owl she's got hundreds of allergies and her mother says she's not to go into dusty places... Well, that upset Brown Owl 'cos our hut is about the dustiest place you could wish for... By the time it was seven-thirty, Lucinda was always out in the loo gasping for breath and coughing. Brown Owl says she's putting it on, and only wants attention. I think it's 'cos Lucinda wants Ruth, Liz, Manda and me out there too, for company. It gets a bit crowded... But as we all want to be nurses when we grow up its good practice as we try to calm her down... I say, "Deep breaths Lucinda...deep breaths." But Ruth says that's not right... (Pause)

Well... Brown Owl set the day for our show... And we all took our pets along... There were lovely prizes and the judges said nice things about all of them... It got a bit more interesting... When Ruth's Billy-goat ate his way through the vicar's plastic Mac... You see, he was bending over Manda's dog basket and his Mac was still sticking out at the back, so the goat started to eat it... Ruth says he'll eat anything! Vicar was a bit annoyed... Then Emma's guinea-pig ran up the church drainpipe... She was showing it to Brown Owl and it

18

just jumped out of her hand... Lucinda got a bit bored 'cos she hadn't brought anything, so she let Liz's Angora rabbit out and it went dashing past Wendy's Old English Sheepdog which was tied to the ice cream stand... The man supposed to be selling the ice cream said something about...'sooing' Brown Owl, and she didn't know how to organise herself properly... But really I blame Lucinda...mind she's left Brownies, she said it was boring... So now she goes with her mother to aerobics at our college... She says it's dust free there...and she really likes aerobics and it helps all her allergies...and she seems OK with her mother...

Things to consider as an actor:

- What do you know about Rainbows and Brownies?
- What is Sophie trying to tell us?
- What happens at the pet show?
- How many moods can you find?

Extension work: Try to find more about allergies.

Vocabulary Building:
What is meant by allergic/rash/Billy goat/vicar/Guinea pig/drainpipe/Angora rabbit/aerobic?

- Remember to think of this as a scene and not just a monologue.
- Tell someone what you think of this character and why.

Notes:

Cobweb with the Indian Boy

This scene is inspired by Shakespeare's *A Midsummer Night's Dream*. Cobweb is seen holding the Indian boy having been given the boy to nurse near the bower in which Titania is sleeping with Bottom. This member of Titania's retinue is taking care of the little boy whilst the Queen is besotted with Bottom who wears the head of an ass.

COBWEB: (Sighing deeply.) So I'm left with the Indian boy... Whilst our Queen drools over her latest love...and a strange headed creature he is, not at all good looking like our King...and certainly not possessing his fine figure and bearing... But it seems she has fallen in love again, and I'm left looking after the boy. (She strokes him fondly and places him tenderly on the ground.) He's sleeping now, tired out after listening to their terrible quarrel, (whispering) terrible rows they have (laughing). Right royal tiffs with foot-stamping, shouting...waving their arms about in a crazy manner... It has quite an effect on the elements... The seasons are all 'topsy-turvy'... Just look at the state of this wood... Who would believe it (pointing) that part over there in Winter, all frozen up and sparkly with frost (Points to another.) and over there we have autumn, all gold and russets, with red hawthorn berries and hazel nuts ready to eat, (Moving to another part of the wood.) and over here summer with the delicate fronds of ferns soft to the touch and honeysuckle scenting the night air... Mmmm! Can you smell it? Mmmm! My favourite scent (breathing in) the scent of summer...lovely (Moving back to the Indian boy). Whilst here, by this Indian boy, the wood is in springtime, offering us the sweet primrose and violets, with everywhere around the boy's sleeping bower bluebells cluster… Oh! He's waking up…hush! (Picking up the boy.) Oh! What will become of you sweet boy? You have such lovely soft skin and such beautiful dark hair. (Nursing the boy.) Our Queen used to dote on you…kiss and cuddle you, but now she lies in the arms of that ugly mortal, smitten by his looks (glancing over to see Tatiana and whispering) the King is so angry with her and who knows what will happen next? (The boy wakes up.) Oh! Hush boy, don't wake up on me. (She rocks the boy and softly sings a lullaby.)

Sleep under the stars little boy
Dream your dreams of glory
Sleep under the stars little boy
And I will tell you a story

(She gently places the boy on the ground again.) Good! That's done the trick… (She looks over at him lovingly as she sits down to watch over him.) Do you know, I don't blame King Oberon wanting him so much… He really is a beautiful Indian boy…

Things to consider as an actor:

- Find out what you can about *Midsummer Night's Dream.*
- Why is the Indian boy so important to the story?
- What do we learn about the wood that Cobweb is in?
- How many moods can you find?

Extension work: Explain what happens to the Indian boy.

Vocabulary Building: What is meant by drools /bearing/fondly/ royal tiffs/ topsy-turvy /russets/ hawthorn berries/hazelnuts/fronds/ferns/honeysuckle/bower/dote/ mortal/smitten/lullaby?

- Remember to think of this as a scene and not just a monologue.
- Tell someone what you think of this character and why.

Notes:

I'm Cheesed Off

This speech will work equally well for a boy or girl. The young person is complaining to a friend. It can be set in a bedroom, with mime suggesting the picking up of clothes and games. Opening drawers and filling boxes can be effective in extending the atmosphere being projected.

JO: Do this! Do that! Tidy this! Clean that! It's like living in a concentration camp. I'm cheesed off! Why can't I be naturally untidy? You want to hear old bossy big- boots talking to her friends. "Oh yes," she says, "I like my children to be individuals... Do their own thing, you know. I just can't abide children with no characters—the cowed type. You know!" Oh, she does go on. Then when she comes home, it's straight up to inspect my bedroom to find out if I've done what I was told!

Well, I admit, it is a bit...untidy...a bit messy... Just the odd ten or twelve books scattered around. The odd three or four games all out of their boxes. (Crawls over the floor.) One or two empty yoghurt cartons, then two or three puzzles not quite finished...and well, clothes look better with wrinkles, don't they? And anyway...they're MY clothes! If I want to pile them on my desk, why can't I? If I want to look a wreck, why can't I? But am I allowed to? No! I'm just not allowed to be myself, EVER!

It's tidy up that bedroom, hang those clothes up, put those games away! Mothers! Why can't they be more like dads?

Things to consider as an actor:

- What is suggested by mentioning a 'concentration camp'?
- Explain what is being suggested by 'the cowed type'?
- Describe Jo's feelings in this scene.
- How many moods can you find?

Vocabulary Building:
What is meant by cheesed off/individuals/abide/look a wreck?

- Remember to think of this as a scene and not just a monologue.
- Tell someone what you think of this character and why.

Notes:

Giving Up

The scene is set in a PE changing room. This allows for a lot of mimed actions suggesting getting changed out of school uniform into their PE kit. Charlie is telling his friend about his violin lessons.

CHARLIE: It's too much of a hassle, right! You have to go up to the music department and check the board to see when your violin lesson is and then tell your subject teacher one week ahead that you'll be missing, isn't it...? Then the lessons are never supposed to take you out of the same subject two weeks running, right! Well, that never works... Well...not for me... I don't know who does that lesson timetable for violins? But I've missed half my history lesson three weeks running...three weeks! I don't know anything about the Black Death except they all went around sneezing themselves to death in three days... And how is that supposed to get me through my history test...and Gareth won't let me borrow his book to copy up because the last time he did that, I lost his book and then he spent hours copying up from Ted's book... And Sir was really nasty to him and gave him a detention.

Really Edward, I never wanted to play the violin, but Mum said that it was her favourite instrument: "And the only one she wanted to hear in our house." I really wanted to play the trombone; there aren't many trombone players around. The music department could do with a trombone player too for our annual Eisteddfod...but no, Mum says: "What! A nasty sounding instrument like a trombone. And they're huge. And they cost a fortune! I'm not having a great big thing like a trombone stuck in the car. How would we get you, that trombone, Suzie, Lucie and Jo in the car? It wouldn't work. And what would the neighbours say about a thing like a trombone blasting through their walls when you're practicing? Mrs Crowe complains enough about your violin practicing on a Sunday morning—the 'Sabbath' to her—so what would she be like complaining about a trombone: demented."

I don't think Mum is thinking about my future. There are hundreds of violin players... But not many trombone players... So if I can't play a trombone, I'm going to tell them I'm giving up learning the violin... I'm not going to play anything... They can sell my violin. And then I can stay in my history lessons and learn about the Black Death... I wonder, if they sell my violin...will Mum give me the money? It is my violin, isn't it? So that's only fair...

OK! So life isn't fair... Don't be so miserable...

Things to consider as an actor:

- Finding out more about what is called 'The Black Death'?
- Exactly what is a trombone; has it got a long history as a musical instrument?
- Explain Charlie's feelings in this scene.
- How many moods can you find?

Vocabulary Building: What is meant by hassle/ Eisteddfod/fortune/Sabbath/demented?

- Remember to think of this as a scene and not just a monologue.
- Tell someone what you think of this character and why.

Notes:

The Search Is On

All the action takes place in Ruth's house just before leaving for het ballet lesson. It is the usual hunt for her ballet shoes for the class. Ruth never knows where she has put them from one lesson to the next. She can be looking under chairs, in drawers, on windowsills, behind curtains; all of which requires mimed action which helps to bring the scene to life. We imagine that the mother too is hunting in another part of the house, but within earshot. Ruth often imitates her mother's voice as part of the dialogue with the unseen.

RUTH: (Calling out) OK Mum, keep your hair on! Stop panicking, will you? My ballet shoes are bound to be here somewhere... They haven't just walked off (frantically searching around) Yes! I know I should have 'a special place where I always keep them' but I clearly haven't... All right! I know we have to leave for my class 'in three minutes' time' just leave me alone... They are bound to be here...somewhere... (Searches on her knees under a chair or sofa.) Oh' what's this? A sweet (examines it) looks all right, wrapper still on, seems untouched by human mouth. (She opens the wrapper.) I would hate it to have been even touched by Darren's hand let alone his mouth. (Pops it in her mouth.) Mmmm nougat, yummeeee...good (shouting out). All right Mum, I'm still looking... You look in the dining room, perhaps they're in the sideboard drawer. (She looks in some drawers herself.) Gosh! It's amazing what you find when you're looking for something else... I haven't seen this Alice band in ages; (shouting out) will you stop shouting, Mum... I am organised... Somebody's moved my ballet shoes...! Bet it's Darren (shouts). Ask Darren, he's always moving my things: "Now why would Darren move your ballet shoes, you should take better care of them, it's always the same, every week," Broken record time...(getting really angry) OK So where are they? Where the heck did I put them? (Suddenly, Ruth's mum appears in the doorway, confronting Ruth)...my ballet shoes! You've found them...what? They were in your car the whole time, under the front seat. (Ruth changes her mood.) Well, don't look at me like that! We've got them now (Marching past Mum and snatching her ballet shoes)... Let's get a move on, Mum, or we'll be late for my class... (Turning to look at Mum)... You don't want me to be late yet again, do you?

Things to consider as an actor:

- What are the origins of ballet?
- Has the modern ballet shoe always been worn?
- Explain Ruth's feelings in this scene.
- How many moods can you find?

Vocabulary Building: What is meant by frantic/nougat/Alice band?

- Remember to think of this as a scene and not just a monologue.
- Tell someone what you think of this character and why.

Notes:

A Witch's Lament

A young witch, who is attending a Witch Training School, is sitting behind a table looking at a book of *Special Potions for Young Witches.* She has failed her latest exam and has been placed on probation.

ADA: Failed again. These potions are so hard to get right. A bit of this, a pinch of that, there's even a potion that says *soupçon* of dried ants! Who writes these potion books? There's one potion recipe that says… (She flicks through the pages)… Here we are (Reads out). "For the biggest effect, take a clutch of Adder skins and stir vigorously!" (She pulls a face.) Now exactly what is a 'clutch'? That's why I keep failing the course… What size is a bit? How much is a pinch? And as for *soupçon*, well I give up… (She slams shut the potion book.) I don't want to grow up to be a witch anyway. But what does Mum say (She mimes her mother), "Ada, your Gran is a witch, I am a witch, and you will be a witch! We have been witches for generations. Way back. FOREVER!" She's like a broken down CD sometimes, just going on and on and on. (Ada gets up from the table.)

What I want is to go to ballet school and do *pliés* (she demonstrates) and twirls (She tries this but topples over.) I could do that if I had time to practice… But no, it's the (Put in any area known to actor.) Witch Training School and I have to wear this stupid hat and cloak when I'd rather be wearing a pink tutu! And you'll never guess what Mum said to me yesterday, (She mimics mother again.) "Ada, your nose needs to grow more pointed. Your chin needs to stick out more! You're far too pretty for a witch. NO ONE will take you seriously. You cannot be a pretty witch." It makes me

miserable; I don't want a horrible pointed nose and chin...
I'm here in witch detention because I turned a bunny rabbit
into a pig instead of a parrot. Too many pinches of something
probably, or too many stirs... Right! Pull yourself together
Ada. (Flicks through her recipe book.) Now, here is a potion
for turning that dove there (Points to an imagined dove on a
stool.) into a tabby kitten... (She puts the book in front of her,
arranges bowls and has various ingredients on the table.) Now
concentrate, Ada. (She reads from the book and mimes the
putting together of all the ingredients for the potion.) Right!
Two pinches of powder of toads. Three pinches of crystallised
bee stings. A bit of aromatic witch hazel. Oh no! A *soupçon*
of dried adder skins and stir with a wooden spoon... Then the
magic chant:

Dubbledee-goo-an-rumatamdoo!

Oh! No! Got that wrong... It's... (Reading carefully)...
Dubble-dubble-doo-an-rumatumdee!

(She waves her hand over the potion bowl.)

Voila! (She stares at an animal she's just created.) Oh no,
no, no! It's a tiger... (She is petrified.) Now be a nice tiger, a
really nice friendly tiger... This is the biggest mistake of my
witch training...

(Ada suddenly falls to the floor as the imagined tiger
jumps up on her.) Get off! Get off!

Things to consider as an actor:

- Which time of year are witches thought to
  congregate?
- Explain Ada's feelings in this scene.
- How many moods are there?

Vocabulary Building:

What is meant by lament/potions/*soupçon*/adder skins
/mimics/generations/plié/tutu/ingredients/crystallised/aromat
ic/witch hazel/voila?

- Remember to think of this as a scene and not just a monologue.
- Tell someone what you think of this character and why.

Notes:

The Wizard's Reproach

Aldo is the Chief High Wizard at a major Wizard's training academy. He is telling off a group of young wizards who have all failed in their end-of-term exam. He is annoyed with them and is trying to motivate them to do better when they re-sit their exam. All the failed wizards are sitting in front of Aldo, who speaks to them directly, his eyes sweeping around the room.

ALDO: All of you! Yes, all of you have failed yourselves and me. What a shower of abject failures… This is the worst year this academy has ever been saddled with… (He scowls at them.) All you seem to be interested in is laughing and joking… And you laugh even louder when you get it wrong! (He points at one of the young wizards.) You! Sandro Angromovitch, all the way from Moscow, turned a white dove into a broomstick instead of a white rabbit…why are you all laughing at that? Mm? It is a catastrophe! And you can stop smirking Sandro as it is not funny… Smirking is absolutely forbidden! Is that the sort of behaviour you go in for in Russia when you fail your exams? (He glares at them.) And as for you Carlo Carluccio, all the way from the Venetian Junior Academy of Wizardry… You turned your white dove into a tin of biscotti… (Enraged) A tin of biscotti! Don't any of you laugh! This is no laughing matter… You are all here to learn the Art of Wizardry and up until now we have always had a 100% pass rate… At the last Ofsted inspection, we were rated excellent! But all that is being eroded…yes! Eroded by your slack, slipshod and lackadaisical manner… All right Carlo Carluccio, you will have to look all those words up in your dictionary… OK so you have a smart phone. Don't start using your iPhone now Carlo, just watch me demonstrate how you turn a white dove into a white rabbit...all of you pay attention... Sandro! Will you put that iPhone away before I confiscate it...yes! I know you would like to know what slipshod is in Russian...but it can wait... Right!

All eyes on me...concentrate...

(Aldo goes into a complicated ritual of rolling up his sleeves, miming getting a pot for his potion, collecting a wand to wave and placing an imagined dove on a table after taking it out of its cage. He then opens a Potions Manual and the lid of his ingredients box.)

Page 206 clearly states... (He takes various ingredients from his box and throws them into the pot.) A pinch of toad skin, a pinch of cow dung (agh!) 2 spoons of goat's milk, a twirl of black pepper and a sprinkle of ginger cat's fur and then (Waving his wand around)...

Abbracadabracumstandatoodo!

Zoom (Pointing his wand triumphantly and sprinkling the potion onto the table...) there is a white rab... A packet of spaghetti! SPAGHETTI!

Stop laughing you lot! I forbid it! (He is furious.) Carlo Carluccio... COME HERE!

Things to consider as an actor:

- What do we expect wizards to be like?
- What is Aldo trying to do?
- How would you explain his behaviour?
- Explain Aldo's feelings in this scene.
- How many moods are there?

Vocabulary Building: What is meant by reproach/scowls/catastrophe/smirking/biscotti/eroded/slack/slipshod/lackadaisical/confiscate/potion?

- Remember to think of this as a scene and not just a monologue.
- Tell someone what you think of this character and why.

Notes:

A Hamster Tale

In this scene, Claire is telling her friends at lunchtime in school about the drama at home! They are eating their packed lunches in the designated area.

CLAIRE: Dad was really bad tempered this morning...all grouchy...and he had it in for me... Mum says I always rub him up the wrong way...but I don't...well, if I do sometimes, I don't know I'm doing it... I can't help it if he's touchy, can I? Anyway, when I go to bed, I always take Snuggles up with me... He's a really cute hamster not one of those 'bite your finger off hamsters'...you know... The really nasty ones which really dig their nasty little front teeth into your hand... Emma's got one like that called Sparky...yeah... An' he's really, really nasty an' she says he's no fun, not like my Snuggles an' she says she'd like to do a swap...but I'd never part with him... I love sitting in my bedroom and watch him spin around in his little wheel...round and round he goes as happy as can be... The cutest little hamster in the world...

Oh! Yeah, why was Dad mad at me? Well, last night, I took Snuggles out of his cage and snuggled him down with me under the duvet...now usually I do it for about ten minutes, then I put him back in his cage...after I've given him a big kiss... But last night, I was so tired after Brownies* that I went to sleep with Snuggles under the duvet...fast asleep... Well of course, he got out and went exploring... Dad was fast asleep and something ran over his face...and he woke up an' there was nothing there... So he went back to sleep... And then a bit later, something ran over his face an' he shot up in bed thinking it was a rat! 'Cos the 'thing' had claws...an' then he saw Snuggles looking at him, made a grab for him but he ran off…and Dad thought, *Hell! The cat…the cat will get Snuggles.* So he jumped out of bed… Then Snuggles ran out of the bedroom and down the stairs with Dad after him… Mum slept through all this drama, once she goes to sleep she's out of it…and Snuggles runs all around the place downstairs with Dad trying to catch him before the cat could get to him… And it lasts for hours… Then he finally corners Snuggles in the kitchen and makes a grab for him…but Snuggles is now like 'mega-frightened' and when Dad gets hold of him, he bites him… Well, he's never bitten me… So Dad drops him…and Snuggles is now very, very frightened so he runs under the fridge…and Dad has to wait for him to come out…and it all takes hours… But he does get him…and puts him in his cage… But Dad hasn't had a good night's sleep…and then he goes back to bed…goes to sleep…but wakes up again…because the cat is locked outside and is meowing his head off outside the bedroom window…'cos he wasn't in the house at all…and Dad blames me for everything!

I'm not flavour of the month at the moment.

(*This can be substituted for any activity suitable to the age of the actor.)

Things to consider as an actor:

- What sort of relationship does Claire appear to have with her dad?
- What can you find out about hamsters?
- Explain Claire's feelings in this scene.
- How many moods are there?

Vocabulary Building: What is meant by grouchy/ touchy/snuggle/duvet/drama/mega-frightened?

- Remember to think of this as a scene and not just a monologue.
- Tell someone what you think of this character and why.

King Panto's Violin

In this scene, set in a market square, the King's Secretary has an important announcement to make. Organizitwell could be played by either a boy or girl. Organizitwell is rather pompous. A suggestion of costume might help, such as a feathered cap and cloak.

ORGANIZITWELL: Line them up, guards; line them up. That's it, straight lines and hats off. Now the King has ordered that every male over the age of sixteen must be interrogated. Why? You mean, you don't know? This morning, as King Panto was playing his violin, he put it down in the Royal Rose Garden, and lo and behold, after he'd finished blowing his nose, (very particular he is about his nose) it had gone. Gone! His magic violin not his nose. It plays in tune, however awful the royal fingers stumble, perfect tune. Mozart it plays, Beethoven, Schu... Ah! Well, your sort of person wouldn't know, would you? Keep in line, keep in line.

The King was so upset, he couldn't eat his usual breakfast of four bowls of chocolate chips with orange sauce, four pieces of Black Forest Gateau and two wedges of fruit cake. Instead, he only managed a box of Turkish delight and a strawberry milkshake. Now, he has commissioned me to find the thieves who stole the Royal violin. Who am I? You mean, nincompoops, you don't know who I am? I am Organizitwell, the Royal Secretary. You will address me as Your Secretaryship.

Now, who will be first with information? Come on, someone must know something. If you don't come forward, the King will close all the discos... He will close all the chippies...he will... Come on, confess!

Oh, yes! I forgot to say, there's a £100 reward. Ah! Don't all stampede, stop shouting... One at a time, one at a time please.

(Falls to the ground besieged by informants.)

Things to consider as an actor:

- What kind of imagined land would this character inhabit?
- Draw a sketch of what you think his costume might be like.
- Explain what you think Organizitwell's attitude is like towards the unseen group.
- Explain the secretary's feelings in this scene.
- How many moods are there?

Vocabulary Building: What is meant by interrogated/ stumble/Mozart/Beethoven/Gateau/commissioned/nincompo oops/stampede/besieged/informants?

- Remember to think of this as a scene and not just a monologue.
- Tell someone what you think of this character and why.

Notes:

The Tooth Fairy's Lament

The Tooth Fairy has just completed a full night on duty flying around leaving coins for children who have lost a tooth. She has come to the Tooth Compensation Department office to hand in the two regulatory bags she is issued with—one for teeth and one for compensation coins. She is exhausted and flops down on an office chair to complain about how tough the job is. She is still carrying the two bags. Explore the use of mime, as she engages with the imagined audience.

TOOTH FAIRY: Thank goodness, it is daylight and I can rest my weary wings. (Sits down) What a night! One of the busiest ever, I can tell you… This seems to be the 'Tooth Falling out Season'. I can go for ages coping very well, no hassle, nice and easy…then *WHAM!* (She smacks her hands together.) There are teeth falling out all over the place… Mind, I have my suspicions about some kids… (She gets up and paces the floor.) There are some nasty kids who actually pull their teeth out to get the money! Now, that is simply cheating! A tooth should just fall out, just naturally…but no, some little devils give their wobbly teeth a twist…and… Hey presto! Out it comes… THAT IS CHEATING BIG TIME and it ought to mean: NO VISIT FROM THE TOOTH FAIRY! But, you know, parents wouldn't agree to it…No! Their little darlings must get a visit from the Tooth Fairy or there will be tears… AND WE CAN'T HAVE THAT, CAN WE! (Mocking them.)

(Sitting down again.) My wings are aching with all that flying about. If the Tooth Compensation Department got their act together, they could divide the UK up in to 3 zones… There could be a Welsh Tooth Fairy, Welsh speaking of course, just working in Wales, and a Scottish Tooth Fairy, with tartan wings, working through Scotland... Now wouldn't it make sense? And I could just do England.

And to make things more complicated at night, I never know where the kid has put the tooth... Can you understand my problem? I fly into the bedroom, very quietly, and gently search under the pillow...and there's nothing there! But the child is on my list. The Tooth Compensation Department is never wrong, so there's no mistake...and then I have to madly flit around looking in bowls, boxes, tins, dolly pockets...the tooth could be anywhere...and it all takes time... Sometimes I am a nervous wreck by the time I've found it and leave my coin, and this bag weighs a ton when I start—I really need a Tooth Fairy helper, an assistant... But the Tooth Fairy Compensation Department say they haven't got a big enough budget and they are facing departmental cuts anyway...

Oh! Well, poor me, a victim of budget cuts... I'm off to get some rest. (Gets up) I'll dump these bags on the counter...and then off to get some sleep... Perhaps with a little bit of luck, tonight will not be so busy.

Bye for now! And wish me luck. (Waves)

Things to consider as an actor:

- The purpose of a tooth fairy.
- Draw a sketch of what this character could look like.
- Explain the tooth fairy's feelings in this scene.
- How many moods are there; describe them?

Vocabulary Building:

What is meant by lament
/compensation/regulatory/weary/coping/hassle/presto/
mocking/zones/tartan/madlyflit/weighs
aton/budget/departmental cuts/victim?

- Remember to think of this as a scene and not just a monologue.
- Tell someone what you think of this character and why.

Notes:

The Elf Worker

An elf is in his workshop seated at a table counting Lego blocks into boxes, ready for Santa's Christmas visits. Around him, in his workshop are different boxes and sacks that are to be filled up over the year; ready for the festive delivery. Explore the use of mime to find the emotional levels as the audience is drawn into the thought patterns in this scene.

ELF: (Picking up Lego blocks and counting)... 51, 52, 53, 54, 55, 56, 57, 58. Right! That's another box filled... (He closes the box.) Why there are boxes of 58 Lego pieces and not 60 is a mystery to me... But that's the number I've been told to put into each box and there's a big commotion by the Quality Control Elf if I get it wrong and put in 59! You cannot argue with him... (The Elf gets up and walks around his workshop.) It isn't easy being an Elf worker... All these sacks have to be filled up... I bet you think after Christmas Eve we have nine months off, then a surge of orders in October when that Ice Hotel down the road gets filled up with kids and their parents...easy you think! Nine months off, then a three-month stampede to get things finished for December 24th...but it's not like that at all... I don't lead a sedentary life for months...

The Quality Control Department has to make predictions, so we can get cracking on January 1st every year. There's no peace for elves like me... But, I want promotion to Elf Quality Controller, now they have a great job. They sit and watch toy advertisements being shown to kids during the year and make predictions... They sit there with big mugs of tea and plates of chocolate biscuits and watch the ads...mind you...it's the Chief Elf Quality Controller's job I want really, really, really. He has to watch all the children's DVDs that come out...take

Frozen for example… He says, "That's the one! Make hundreds of lookalike dolls, all those girls are gonna want them for Christmas!" And he was right… It overtook the Barbie doll craze and Santa went off with sacks full of *Frozen* lookalikes. (He returns to his table and start counting Lego blocks again.) 1, 2, 3, 4, 5… Life has got harder since Lapland became a Christmas tourist destination… That Ice Hotel is a magnet…and all these kids have to go and see Santa in his Ice Grotto and give him a letter with their wishes… We work as hard as we can on the 'wish list', and then two weeks before Christmas, they see something on TV and change their minds! It drives me crazy… We worker elves have to work 15-hour shifts to get everything made in time for delivery… Santa will not have children crying 'cos they haven't got what they wanted'… He comes back a bit tipsy. But he brings us loads of mince pies that are left for him… It's mince pie heaven for Elves on Christmas Day… Right! Forget about mince pies…now it's putting Lego blocks into boxes… 6, 7, 8, 9, 10…

Things to consider as an actor:

- Why *Frozen* seems to have a big impact on him?
- Draw a sketch of what this character could look like.
- Explain the Elf's feelings in this scene.
- How many moods are there; describe them?

Vocabulary Building:
What is meant by festive/mystery/commotion/quality control/ surge /ice hotel/ stampede/ sedentary/predictions /Lapland/ ice grotto/ shifts/ tipsy?

- Remember to think of this as a scene and not just a monologue.
- Tell someone what you think of this character and why.

On Safari

A boy or girl is sitting on a bench in a school playground telling their friends what they did at the weekend. Imagine a group, not just one friend. They are eating their mid-morning snack, which will allow for the development of mime actions.

BUZZ: It was actually Dad's idea. He had been saying for a long time that he wanted to go to a Safari Park... 'Cos Mum said she wasn't going to the real thing. You know like go to Africa and see animals in the wild... She's super allergic to mosquitoes... It's bad enough when we go camping in France. Anyway, Mum says that African mosquitoes give people malaria and she's not spending the rest of her life having fever attacks... So Africa is definitely, like, out. So, Dad said, "OK, let's go to that Safari Park we pass on the way to my mother's. We could do the Safari Park, and then go on and have the kids visit their grandma." So Mum's OK with that...sort of... Richie and me get really excited 'cos we think we will see lions and tigers...

When we get there, there's a big, long queue, and Dad's not good with queues. Like he's on a short fuse... Well... Mum calls it 'a short fuse'. He certainly gets fed up quickly... But it's Saturday and there are hundreds of cars all lined up at the entrance...paying... Dad complains about the cost... But Mum says it was 'his' idea so he shouldn't moan... Finally, we get in and there are big notices saying 'Keep Moving' and 'Don't Get out of Your Vehicle'... Mum says, "All these notices spoil it for me..." Dad starts driving through... We're all looking for lions and tigers when we start going under some trees and this monkey drops down onto our bonnet. Mum says, "Oh! Look, isn't he cute. Look at his little face and twinkly eyes…" And this monkey is looking straight at Dad, like eye-balling him and starts to grin… A monkey grin…like this… (Grins broadly) Dad carries on driving and this monkey will not budge… Mind, we are going ever so slowly 'cos of all the cars in front… Ours is the only car with a monkey on the bonnet… Mum says, "It's having a free ride…a monkey ride…"

And Dad says, "I wish it would hop it, just hop off back into the trees…"

But he and Dad are still eye-balling each other, and Mum says, "Oh! He likes you David, he's taken a fancy to you…" and she starts laughing… Dad can't see the funny side and leans forward and starts to tap the windscreen to try and frighten him off… In the end, Dad's banging on the windscreen, but that monkey isn't shifting! Dad's short fuse has busted by now… And at that point, this monkey, looking him straight in the eye, wrenches the windscreen wiper off the window…! Can't repeat what Dad said… Then it looked as if this monkey is killing himself laughing… It's screeching and jumping up and down waving the windscreen wiper like a trophy… Mum doesn't say anything because the monkey is then…then…well…leaving something…like soft and brown all over our bonnet… Richie and I thought Mum and Dad were in a state of shock. They didn't say anything, but stared out of the windscreen…dazed…

We didn't see any lions or tigers… And we didn't go to Gran's afterwards…

Things to consider as an actor:

- What a Safari Park might be like?
- Describe the different attitudes of the mother and father.
- Explain how Buzz feels in this scene.
- How many moods are there?

Vocabulary Building:

What is meant by safari/super allergic/ mosquitoes /malaria/short fuse/eye-balling/trophy/dazed?

- Remember to think of this as a scene and not just a monologue.
- Tell someone what you think of this character and why.

Notes:

The London Zoo Trip

A boy or a girl is telling their school friends about a trip to London Zoo. They are sitting on benches in the schoolyard. The child is a lively storyteller, and the other children are really engaged in this account. They are all eating their mid-morning snacks.

TOZIE: What a weekend... It was a buster! Dad decided to take us to London Zoo... Mum wasn't keen 'cos she thinks wild animals should be out in the wild, not cooped up in small spaces... Mum is really into Animal Rights and how they have feelings too, just like humans... When we had a mouse in the kitchen, she wouldn't let Dad put down poison... He had to go and buy a humane mouse trap... One where the mouse hops in, it isn't killed and you release it outside... I think that mouse came back three times... Then Dad was told you should drive the mouse about five miles down the road and then let it out...he did get a bit fed up in the end...but taking it five miles away did work and we were 'mouse free'... Anyway... We all got ready on Saturday to go to the zoo. When we got to Kings Cross Station, Dad said we needed the Northern line, it's North... But Mum said we needed the Bakerloo line, it's West...but Dad won and we all followed him... We could tell Mum wasn't happy about this... Dad said women have no sense of direction and we needed to go north... Mum said we needed to go west... Well, Claire and I had no idea... So we just trailed along... It was boiling hot on the Underground and they had these announcements about carrying water with you...and not getting on the train if you felt dodgy...like dehydrated.

Of course, we got lost and Mum had a blazing row with Dad on the platform... Claire and I pretended we were not with them...that we belonged to another family... Eventually, after following Mum... By now, Dad was in a foul mood... We got to Baker Street and at the top of the stairs, Mum bought an A to Z of London which she said we should have had in the first place... I thought I heard her say that Dad was 'an old meany-pants' but I can't swear to that...We finally got to the zoo... Claire is too scared to ask to go to the shop and I thought it might be better to ask for an ice cream after things had cooled down a bit...When we got inside, Mum said she wanted to take us to the 'Kids Corner'! I mean, me and Claire 'kids!' I wanted to see elephants, Claire wanted to see giraffes... And Mum stomps off to the 'Kids Corner' with Dad saying he wanted to go to the Snake House... Mind, that 'Kids Corner' was a bit of a laugh... There was a man leaning over a fence watching some rare-breed chickens when this goat went up behind him and started eating his plastic Mac... It looked like rain... it chewed up the back and the man didn't know... Mum said, "Goats will eat anything," but plastic Mac stuff can't be healthy for a goat, can it? And goats shouldn't be allowed to just roam around like that...

Dad went up to this man and said, "Excuse me, there's a goat eating your plastic Mac..." And when he turned 'round... He looked like a Chinese tourist and he didn't have a clue as to what Dad was saying...really bewildered...! Think he thought Dad was trying to sell him something...well, it made us all laugh... And then we went to the Snake House... Dad was pleased... It was a family day out and we saw this huge anaconda... Huge it was! Like this...(holds arms out at full length).

Things to consider as an actor:

- What seems to be the relationship between the mother and father?
- What can you find out about London Zoo?
- Explain Tozie's feelings in this scene.

- How many moods are there?

Vocabulary Building:
What is meant by cooped up/dodgy/dehydrated/foul mood/stomps off/roam around/anaconda?

- Remember to think of this as a scene and not just a monologue.
- Tell someone what you think of this character and why.

Notes:

Food

This speech is suitable for either sex. Pat is talking to a school friend, whilst doing some homework. The performer could also mime eating or watching TV; try to explore all the mime possibilities.

PAT: All this talk about junk food. Well, let's get one thing straight, I like junk food, crisps, chips, beef burgers, what's wrong with 'em. And white bread, why can't I have sliced white bread from the supermarket? It's all food, isn't it? But no... Mum's into high fibre diets, it's enough to kill you... Wholemeal bread, great big chunks of it...yuck! And no one's allowed butter anymore... That's supposed to be a real killer.

Well... My mum made Dad give up smoking 'cos it's a killer an' he did it, just to please 'er... Now he's got to give up butter, cheese, streaky bacon and cream puddings... They're all killers... How the human race has survived so far, I'll never know... My gran says she's not giving up butter even if it is going to kill 'er... But I reckon at seventy-eight, she's got to be immune to whatever it is what kills you in butter.

We get all these colour magazines about health foods. If I see another bean salad, I'm going to be sick all over the place...yuck...and jacket potatoes covered in yoghurt...yuck... Gran an' me, we sneak down to the chippy an' get a great big bag of chips... She meets me after Youth Club.

Mum's now counting cups of coffee... We're only allowed one cup after each meal 'cos more is supposed to be bad for you... Gran spends most of her time down the cafe drinking cups of coffee an' smoking herself silly between cream cakes... I bet she regrets coming to live with us... But then, that was before Mum got hooked on high fibre... I wonder how long before all these killers get to Gran? That's the worrying bit...

Things to consider as an actor:

- Finding out more about what is called 'Junk Food'.
- Explain Pat's feelings in this scene.
- How many moods are there?

Vocabulary Building: What is meant by high fibre diets/wholemeal bread/immune?

- Remember to think of this as a scene and not just a monologue.
- Tell someone what you think of this character and why.

Notes:

Orange

The scene is set in a school-dining hall where two girls are having their mid-morning break. During the scene, Linda is drinking and snacking as she talks to her friend. Explore all the mime opportunities.

LINDA: (Drinking) Oh! I needed that. I was feeling really 'dehydrated'…yeah! Christy, I could have said 'thirsty' but I like the sound of dehydrated ever since we had that lesson on how drinking water helps you keep concentrated…(drinks again) mind… I'll tell you what keeps me concentrating at the moment…me in orange… Can you imagine me dressed in orange with hair this colour. (She touches her hair.) It's bad enough being made to wear a uniform that's brown with yellow edging without being made to wear orange… A dress in orange satin and chiffon… I ask you Christy…what bride in her right mind would want her bridesmaids in a colour like orange when there are all those lovely shades of pink she could go for…honestly… Like she's out of it…and it's doing my head in.

When Mum said my Auntie Pam was finally getting married… I thought 'great'!

I've always wanted to be a bridesmaid… OK Christy so you've been 'A bridesmaid three times' there's no need to brag about it…OK! OK! So, you wore 'Blue for the first two' and 'Pink for the third'. OK Lucky you! Show off!

Mum says, "But it's a summer wedding, so orange will look really pretty and if it's dull and overcast, you'll brighten the day up!" What is she on? Brighten the day up…five of us all in orange with orange frills… She says it's no good arguing with her 'cos Auntie Pam has made her mind up and that's the colour she wants... She actually told Mum it's her favourite colour... Can you believe it? And we're all supposed to have bouquets made up of some flower called Freesia 'cos you can get them in a deeper orange... OK so you've never heard of Freesias... And you'll love this touch Christy... They are having orange slipperettes made for us...yuck!

And mega-yuck! Yes, you are so right, I hope it doesn't rain... Just think of what I'll look like... And wait for this... The finishing touch from Auntie Pam... An orange satin Alice-band with orange silk Freesias sewn down one side and flopping over my left ear! I am going to look awful.

What are you laughing about? Is it the colour of my hair with an orange Alice-band stuck in it.

Try to consider as an actor:

- The importance of bridesmaids in a wedding: why do you think they are important?
- Draw a sketch of what Linda might look like at Auntie Pam's wedding.
- Explain how Linda is feeling in this scene.
- How many moods are there?

Vocabulary Building: What is meant by dehydrated/ satin/ chiffon/brag/ overcast/ Freesias/ slipperettes/ Alice-band?

- Remember to think of this as a scene and not just a monologue.
- Tell someone what you think of your character and why.

Notes:

April 1ˢᵗ, School Trip

The scene is set outside the school gates. Lexy wears a backpack and also carries a plastic bag. The school trip to a Rare Breeds Farm has just returned and parents are collecting their children. Think of all your mime opportunities.

LEXY: Hello, Mum! Of course, I've got mud all over my trainers… It's 'cos it was our farm visit today… How could you forget? Yes! Remember… It was to Leigh Wood Rare Breeds Farm out on Ridge Road… We got a letter, didn't we…remember… Mum! What planet are you on? Sometimes you're not really with it…the letter said 'April 1ˢᵗ is our visit to a rare breed's farm and it will be an all-day event'. Remember! OK! OK! Don't go off your rocker… So you forgot…

Yeah! It was fine… And we saw these huge cows with horns out here (Lexy raises arms to show the extent.) they were massive…! Wouldn't like to meet one of those in the dark… They had shaggy coats to keep them warm and Sir said they come from Scotland and have to keep warm in the Highlands… He said they have the longest hair of any breed of cattle…yeah! We did all remember it was April Fool's Day… In fact, we all had a bit of a laugh about it…you see, Sir was leaning over the fence of this pigsty talking about these pigs we were all supposed to be looking at…big pigs called Gloucester Old Spotted…yeah! Big black spots, all spotty… OK Mum: "SPOTTED." Well, Sir was telling us it was a peasant animal and kept in the orchards so it could feed off the apples that fell off the trees… He got really interested in these pigs… But as he was telling us this Billy goat…NO! Mum, I don't know what breed! It came up behind him and started eating its way up the back of his plastic Mac...you know Mum, Sir wears this really old fashioned see-through plastic Mac... It must be vintage... Like vintage 60s or something... He told us to bring wet-weather clothes...anyway, this Billy goat was really enjoying eating it...like chomping through the back of it and Sir didn't know...

Well, I put my hand up and said, "Sir! Sir!"

And he said, "Put your hand down Lexy, wait 'till I've finished..."

Then Roger put his hand up and said, "Sir! Sir!"

And Sir got fed-up and said, "All of you put your hands down and listen to my information..."

But Roger shouted out: "There's a Billy goat eating your plastic Mac, Sir! Really Sir!"

But Sir just laughed and said; "Oh yeah! Try to play an April Fool's trick on me, eh? Don't think you can get away with it. I'm too smart for you lot! Let's all got to see the bantams. Now some of those are really rare..." And then he turned around and the goat turned around with him, and Sir walked off...and Mum... That goat was still eating his plastic Mac...

And we were all killing ourselves with laughter...

Try to consider as an actor:

- What Rare Breed Farms are trying to do?
- Choose three rare breed animals you like and write about them.
- Explain how Lexy is feeling in this scene?
- How many moods are there?

Vocabulary Building:
What is meant by planet/off your rocker/shaggy coats/peasant/orchards/Billy goat/chomping/bantams?

- Remember to think of this as a scene and not just a monologue.
- Tell someone what you think of your character and why.

Notes:

The Reluctant Shopper

A scene set at home. The boy can be made to mime any suitable game appropriate to his age, whilst speaking the lines, be inventive.

JIM: What a day. It isn't fair, being the only boy in the family means I'm swamped by the girls. There's Mum, then Jane and Esther, three of them! I'm completely out-numbered… This morning, I said, "Can't we go to the Science Museum?" But straight away, the girls look bored. Instant boredom descends the moment I mention a museum… I can't help it if I want to be educated, I want to know things… And the Science Museum is educational, isn't it?

Anyway, what does Mum say, "But it's sales time, and the girls need dresses and new shoes. We haven't got time for museums."

So I say, "All right, you go and I'll watch TV." Mum shakes her head, and says she doesn't trust me, that I'll fiddle with something, set fire to the place, do something awful. It isn't fair. She trusts the girls, they can do what they please…but she calls me 'A right little fiddler'…

So off we go to the shops… Sixteen we must have gone into looking for dresses, and ten shoe shops… Why must there be a shoe shop in every street? It's crazy. Now Jane has squat flat, big feet for her age, and Esther has narrow flat small feet for a five-year-old, and Mother, well she's a treble E fitting, which means that most shops don't stock anything, but round and round we have to go… I call it 'The Big Search for the Treble E's'… Dead boring it is. And they won't look in the shop windows I'm interested in, we zoom past any shops that boys might find interesting. Dad's real clever. He's always got something vital to do at work, top priority. Yes, I know, top priority to get out of shopping! And that lands me in it...

Next time, I'm forced to go with them I'm going to have pains somewhere, in my stomach, or my legs. Mind, I've tried that before... And Mum says, "Oh! Yes, growing pains. You'll have to get used to those. Just be brave." I tell you, you can't win... When the women want a male escort, they'll not take no for an answer. I just wish it could be Dad. After all, they are his responsibility... He shouldn't be let off the hook... It isn't fair...

Try to consider as an actor:

- Why this shopper might be so reluctant?
- Explain how Jim is feeling in this scene?
- How many moods are there?

Vocabulary Building:

What is meant by swamped/educational/squat/treble E/zoom past/vital/priority/escort/off the hook?

- Remember to think of this as a scene and not just a monologue.
- Tell someone what you think of your character and why.

Notes:

The Problem Boy

The scene is set in the interview room of a school psychologist. The boy is trying to explain why he is difficult to teach. He finds it difficult to just sit down and reflect on his behaviour, but nervously moves around as he talks.

CRAIG: Sometimes I like being in school, it's OK... But then I get days when I don't want to bother, everything seems pointless... My foster mother is all right most of the time, she's keen for me to get a good education... She says life's easier if you get a good education; like you end up doing something clever like becoming a psychologist, instead of doing all the donkey work for someone... Yeah I play my radio all night... Well, I can't sleep, can I? Am I supposed to feel sorry for Carl 'cos he can't sleep? He's the other side of a wall, so he should be able to sleep... I play to give me something to do... It isn't funny lying there all night thinking... I mean, Carl's not abandoned by his mother... His mother hasn't gone off with an American... I took my trousers off in Mr Sawford's lesson for a bit of a laugh...

Well, I had my tennis shorts on underneath! He was so busy showing us the Brecon Beacons he didn't notice me wriggling; he didn't turn 'round 'til I had them around my ankles—my trousers—then he started to play hell! He must have known his description of the Brecon Beacons wasn't making Karen and Lisa laugh their heads off... I don't know why I did it... It was a joke... Mind, I thought he was going to wring my neck, but he just ordered me to stand outside the door and confiscated the trousers... You know he threw them in the bin... In the bin with the rubbish! He was in a right rage and it wasn't 'Road Rage'.

All right, so it wasn't the sort of behaviour for a boy of my age… He got his own back didn't he, making me stand outside in the corridor in my tennis shorts an' the Head came along an' made a big fuss…as always… Perhaps I did it 'cos Mrs Bailey smashed my coffee mug that morning… Let it slip she did, right out of her hand. My mum gave me that mug the Christmas before she left us… It had my name on, an' she dropped it. So, I shouted at her… Well, she gets paid by the Council for fostering me, I'm just a business arrangement, it saves her going out to work, doesn't it? Don't try to tell me it's anything different than a business arrangement between Mrs Bailey and Social Services…

Perhaps I do prefer women teachers… The ones here let you get away with murder… It's the men that nag in this school. God! They never stop going on an' on an' on! And Mr Sawford gets the prize for being 'Mr Boring Man of the Year' or 'Boring Teacher of the Year'… I just switch off sometimes…

Try to consider as an actor:

- Is the idea of fostering vulnerable children a good idea or not?
- What do we find out about Craig's feeling in this scene?
- How many moods are there?

Vocabulary Building:
What is meant by psychologist/wring my neck/confiscated/road rage/social services/switch off?

- Remember to think of this as a scene and not just a monologue.
- Tell someone what you think of your character and why.

Passing the Buck

The scene is anywhere, street, sitting room, anywhere a boy might have a chat. It could even be a bowling alley with appropriately mimed actions.

BEN: We have a school trip every year, mind it's got to be educational. They're not going to take us off to the seaside with our bucket and spades... It's got to be work-sheets, and projects...something historical. This year it was Lincoln. Well, that's a good place, castle one side of a hill, an' on the other, this massive cathedral.

The journey up was quite eventful...the other coach, that's Mr Sawford's coach broke down an' our coach had to stop. The coach driver wanted to stick another 48 on our coach, but Mr Sawford wouldn't have it 'cos of health and safety reasons. Whilst all this was happening, someone put a double chew of bubble gum on Gary's coach seat an' when he came back from behind the tree, he'd found when Sir finally let him off the coach, he sat in it, and got it spread all over his backside, an' the seat. The coach driver got all stroppy, an' wanted to wring somebody's neck. He said those coach seats cost £400 a time to be re-upholstered an' he was going on a deluxe tour of Austria in two days' time... Well, when he calmed down a bit he scraped it off with his penknife... An' it was OK... But Gary was going mental...

When we got to Lincoln, they marched us first of all to the castle, motte and bailey it is, I think... We was allowed to go 'round in fours... We had worksheets... Sir said we wasn't to do everything at the gallop... But Gary was running along the wall when he got his blazer caught on a hook what was sticking out…the main bit got separated from the sleeves, sort of…

The Cathedral was fantastic… You could easily lose Sir… The girls spent most of the time in the Cathedral shop… But Gary an' me pretended we was medieval stonemasons carving gargoyles… Sir didn't believe us an' said Gary was defacing holy places… He crept up on us all of a sudden like… Fortunately, at that time, I was watching Gary do his bit of gargoyling, so I pretended I was innocent… Sir marched us all out of the cathedral then… An' it was raining… An' made us do a street survey… Like look at all the funny shaped houses what make up the old parts of Lincoln. Most of the girls wanted ice creams 'stead of filling out forms… They said, "Architecture is boring…" Then Gary put is lollipop what he didn't want down Linda's neck an' she was so busy twisting and screaming that she fell of the kerb, sprained her ankle, put her knee through her tights, tore her blouse and dropped her unfinished 99 special in the middle of the road… It was pandemonium then…

Sir said Gary wasn't to come on any more educational trips, an' next time his education would take place behind a desk at school…so on the way back, he poured a whole bottle of coke, bit by bit into Sir's briefcase. At the moment, they're considering sending him to another school, but I call that 'passing the buck'… They say that Gary's 'on the spectrum' whatever that means…

Try to consider as an actor:

- Why school trips are important?
- What do we find out about Ben's feelings in this scene?
- How many moods are there?

Vocabulary Building:
What is meant by health and safety reasons /stroppy /re-upholstered/deluxe/ going mental/ motte and bailey/

cathedral/ medieval/ gargoyles/ architecture/ pandemonium/
passing the buck/on the spectrum?

- Remember to think of this as a scene and not just a
  monologue.
- Tell someone what you think of your character and
  why.

Notes:

A Christmas Story

This scene is set in the mid-morning break time in school. Georgie speaks to several fellow pupils who are all eating their snacks and drinking. Explore all the mime possibilities that this might offer the actor.

GEORGIE: Dad says he wants to forget Christmas, well it wasn't actually the best we've ever had. Christmas Eve we always go to midnight Mass. The parish church is crammed with people we don't know, and there's always one or two drunks... This year, there was more than two! Vicar didn't look 'full of Christmas spirit' when he came out of the vestry, but a good few of the congregation were full of spirits. Three had to go out for shouting things, and there were two boys smoking behind the Missionary stall; they got pushed out too. Then, when we finally got outside after the service, someone had gone along the street and pulled all the windscreen wipers off the cars... Dad said it must have been the smokers did it for spite... He wasn't filled with Christmas spirit either, and Mum had to remind him that Gran was with us...

By this time, it was raining, and Dad had to drive home peering between fifty million raindrops on the windscreen...he nearly went straight through the garage door. We always get straight into bed, which suited me and Jake, because Dad was in an awful mood, and it was late... I think we should give midnight Mass a miss...

We got up quite late... While we were having breakfast Raffles climbed the Christmas tree thinking the fairy was a bird... Raffles is our cat. Well, that came toppling over... It toppled right on top of Dad's clock... It took him quite a long time to put the bits and pieces back together again, and the chime doesn't work anymore. We lost quite a number of ornaments too...

Raffles got frightened with all the shouting, and hid on the stairs, just by the bend. Gran wanted to know what all the noise was... She never puts any lights on, 'cos she wants to save us money... Well, as she came around the bend in the stairs she fell over Raffles, crashed downstairs, demolished the telephone table and the coat stand and flattened the umbrella stand... Gran's a big woman... She must be all of sixteen stone... We got the car out, then Dad remembered the window wipers... It rained all the way to the hospital. Dad got pretty tense, what with Gran's groaning and not being able to see straight...

We all went with Gran. Mum forgot she had the turkey in the oven, so when we got back finally, it was quite a bit burnt. Raffles didn't seem to mind burnt turkey, she ate quite a lot of it actually... And purred the whole time...

Gran was in hospital five days, and the doctors said she had a lucky escape. Me and Jake don't know what she escaped from, but the doctors never tell you what really is wrong... Dad says 'something always happens at Christmas'. Me and Jake hope he won't be disappointed next year... But Gran says she's staying in her own home... She says it's safer there...

Try to consider as an actor:

- Why is Christmas seen by many people as important?
- What do we find out about Georgie's feelings in this scene?
- How many moods are there?

Vocabulary Building:

What is meant by midnight Mass/parish church/ crammed/vicar/missionary-stall/vestry/congregation/chime/ demolished?

- Remember to think of this as a scene and not just a monologue.
- Tell someone what you think of your character and why.

Notes:

Ancestors

This story-telling to an imagined audience of other friends can be after school with appropriate activities suitable for the actor: explore the mime opportunities.

SANDIE: Our history teacher's keen on ancestors... He says, "How many of you watch Who Do You Think You Are?" Well, about five of us put our hands up... I think he was a bit disappointed... But he says, "It's a great way to identify with the past." And Mandy whispers to me she'd much rather learn about the Romans... But we did the Romans last term... Sir says tracing our ancestors is going to be our project, and we will learn interview skills and have to go off and interview our grandparents... Well, three of my grandparents are dead so it limits it a bit for me... He handed out a list of possible questions to ask...

So last Saturday, I went around to Mum's mum, my granny Sue, for our first interview... Sir said it might take several visits... At the beginning, she wasn't keen to answer my questions... She said 1938 wasn't a good year to be born and later, Germans were dropping bombs and then she had to be evacuated with all the children from her street...she said she cried her eyes out when her mother put her on the train and she didn't like the family who collected her at the other end... I could tell she was getting upset; "Best forgot! Best forgot!" She kept saying... And I really thought she'd start crying... Well, after she'd calmed down, she went and found this old photograph album... Most of them were a funny brown colour... She cheered up a bit when she said her mother had worked as a typist in the city and went to work in a hobble-skirt which was so narrow they had to hobble along like this (Gives a demonstration.) with their knees tied together under the skirt... And they had a terrible time getting on trams... I was laughing, Gran was laughing... But I was thinking what a stupid fashion... I'm glad we don't tie our knees together... After that we got down to some names and dates... We got to look at some ladies wearing fantastic looking dresses all screwed up at the back... Gran said they were called 'bustles' and I thought they probably had a problem when they wanted to sit down...it was a pity it was only in black and white but Gran said they didn't have colour photographs in 1870... Then she took it out to see what was on the back and it was 'Eliza Whitwell married to Thomas Whitwell, Cordwainer' and she said that's my great-granny, and it's your great-great-granny...

I suppose these 'great-greats' could go on forever as I've just started on 'Who Do You Think You Are?' Now I wonder what a 'Cordwainer' is. And how many 'greats' I will end up with...

Try to consider as an actor:

- Why Who Do You Think You Are? Is a popular TV programme?
- Explain the difference between Ancestors and Descendants.
- What do we find out about Sandie's feelings in this scene?
- How many moods are there?

Vocabulary Building:
What is meant by Romans/evacuated/typist-in-the-city/hobble skirt/trams/bustles/Cordwainer?

- Remember to think of this as a scene and not just a monologue.
- Tell someone what you think of your character and why.

Finding a Family Pet

The scene is set in school during the mid-morning snack break with two pupils eating their snack and having a drink. Be inventive with your mime sequences.

BARNEY: Yeah! It was a great weekend... Well, sort of... It had its up and down... We went to this dog show in Birmingham... A really big one... Dad said it was the most important dog show of the year... "Why?"... "Why did we go?"... It's because we are going to get a dog... Nick and I have been nagging for a dog for years... I mean every family needs a pet, don't they? But Mum and Dad can't agree on what sort...big...small...brown...white... You know, all those sort of things... And Mum said, "She's not walking a mongrel and it's got to be pedigree."

Dad wanted a rescue dog... Mum said, "It's 'cos he's mean with his money and didn't want to pay a breeder for a puppy."

She said we might end up, "With a completely traumatised, neurotic dog that we couldn't trust or control." Dad wouldn't listen and so he dragged us all around this rescue centre and honestly... All the dogs did was bark their heads off...mind, they all wagged their tails... But in the end, Mum won 'cos she said she didn't like the look of any of them... Although, Dad liked this big bouncy German Shepherd dog he saw, but Mum said no... And when she says 'No!' it's no!

So we went off to Birmingham... You can't imagine what it was like... This big hall all sectioned off with different parts...like for 'Gundogs and Retrievers' and 'Sheepdogs and Cattle Herders' and all these different showing rings for the

69

breeders to walk their dogs around…and the racket… Well, it was noisy I can tell you. Then Dad spots this sign that says 'Spitz and other Primitive Breeds' so he says, "Come on, that's the one for us" and off we go, thinking Mum is behind us… And we come to this stall and this breeder is combing a Siberian Husky and Dad says, "That's the dog for me, a Man's Dog."

And the breeder says, "If you don't intend to cycle with the dog for at least an hour a day, then forget this breed."

And Dad says, "Not a problem." And I'm thinking, *He's got to be joking 'cos my dad is a mega couch potato… He doesn't move for hours…*

So we go to find Mum, 'cos she went off in another direction and we find her in the 'Toy and other Miniature Dogs' section talking to a breeder about buying this fluffed up white dog with a big pink bow on its head and really small…called a 'Maltese'… And she says, "Isn't she cute? Isn't she lovable?" and she's all sort of gooey and they start arguing straight away… With Dad wanting a Husky and Mum wanting a Maltese that's cute…

And I'm thinking, *No way am I cycling an hour each day with a Husky, and no way am I going to be seen walking a white fluffy thing with a bow in its head…*

Perhaps a rabbit in a hutch would solve the problem? Watch this space to find out who wins…

Try to consider as an actor:

- Using an illustrated book of dogs to find out about the different breeds mentioned in the script.
- What do we find out about Barney's feelings in this scene?
- How many moods are there?

Vocabulary Building:

What is meant by dog show/mongrel/pedigree/rescue dog/traumatised/neurotic/racket/Spitz/primitive breeds/mega couch potato?

- Remember to think of this as a scene and not just a monologue.
- Tell someone what you think of your character and why.

Notes:

Five Duologues for Young Actors

Squirrels' Delight

The scene is set in a garden alongside a main road. Two squirrels are watching a gardener planting tulip bulbs (which are a squirrel delicacy) into pots ready for the spring. The scene involves lively physicality and facial responses so that the unseen world around them is indicated. Finger mime will be an important element.

BOBBI: (He is digging a hole for a nut when Twitcher appears out of breath.) Hey! The last time we met, you said you were going to stay on the other side of that road.

TWITCHER: I know. But Mrs Blondy's hazelnut tree is on this side. Your side... (He tries to calm down.) My side is full of apple trees.

BOBBI: That road is a killer. You'd better be careful.

TWITCHER: Yeah! Tell me about it. I was very upset when Scrappi got squashed.

BOBBI: (Digging another hole.) Flattened by a huge truck.

TWITCHER: Those truck drivers pay no attention to the 'Slow Down' sign at all. They ought to be squashed themselves.

BOBBI: I didn't know you could read?

TWITCHER: No! I can't. But I heard Mrs Blondy talking about it and pointing. She's afraid of being squashed too.

BOBBI: There's more fuss made when humans get squashed...

TWITCHER: Do you know they left Scrappi out there for weeks getting more and more flattened by trucks... (Twitcher begins to get very upset so Bobbi has to console him.)

BOBBI: (Putting his arm around Twitcher.) I know it isn't fair. If a hedgehog gets squashed, they say, "Oh! Look, another dead hedgehog and you know they are an endangered species. The only hedgehogs we see are dead ones. Something needs to be done..."

TWITCHER: (Still upset) I know. And when it's us they say, "Good! Squirrels are only tree rats in fur coats..."

BOBBI: Look, have one of my biggest hazelnuts and bury it for yourself. (He hands Twitcher a nut.) Just make sure there's nothing coming down that hill when you come over for it.

TWITCHER: (Buries the nut.) Do you think you could spare another one?

BOBBI: OK (Hands him one.) but don't push your luck Twitcher.

(Twitcher buries the second nut.) All of a sudden, they both freeze. They speak in whispers.

BOBBI: There's Mrs Blondy. She's come out with a bag and a digger.

TWITCHER: She doesn't like me! She's always shouting at me when I'm on the bird feeder.

BOBBI: Those birds are spoilt rotten.

TWITCHER: They get fresh nuts every day.

BOBBI: And fat balls.

TWITCHER: Spoiled little stuck-up feathered things.

BOBBI: They don't even need to search for food.

TWITCHER: And she feeds them all winter.

BOBBI: Those birdfeeders are hell to get in to. It isn't worth bothering. I can ruin my teeth trying to break in to get those peanuts.

TWITCHER: Stick to hazelnuts mate. (They stop whispering and relax.)

BOBBI: Phew! She's gone inside (He turns to Twitcher.) you know what time of year it is, don't you?

TWITCHER: I know it's getting colder and I have to increase my nut collecting and digging skills...

BOBBI: Yeah! But it's tulip-planting time...

TWITCHER: Tulip bulbs. Oh! I dream about tulip bulbs—yumeee, delicious, scrumptious, tulip bulbs...

BOBBI: Well, Mrs Blondy just planted six...

TWITCHER: I didn't know you could count?

BOBBI: I just guessed. Are you up for this? (He looks at Twitcher.) She's gone in for a coffee.

TWITCHER: So?

BOBBI: We nip down to that place they call 'the patio' and grab ourselves a tulip bulb each before she makes it harder for us...

TWITCHER: What do you mean 'harder'?

BOBBI: Well, last year she covered the top of the pot with holly branches. Nasty spiky stuff. I couldn't get at the tulip bulbs without getting spiked...

TWITCHER: That sounds painful. We could just dig up daffodil bulbs...

BOBBI: Twitcher! Didn't your mother tell you that daffodil bulbs are poisonous? We have to avoid daffodil bulbs at all costs. Killers they are. KILLERS! (He gets really upset.) That's why Mrs Blondy doesn't bother to cover them with anything. She knows they are safe.

TWITCHER: So, are we going to make a grab for them?

(They get themselves ready to dash down to the patio area. Once there they drag through the compost searching for tulip bulbs. It is a mad scramble, but they finally get one each and run up the garden to a safe spot away from the patio.)

BOBBI: OK Twitcher, (out of breath) this bush is great for hiding under.

TWITCHER: I don't think I would have been brave enough without you.

BOBBI: Right! So let's each dig a hole; (Looking at his bulb.) it's got to be ten times the size of a hazelnut hole.

TWITCHER: That's a hell of a lot of hole, Bobbi.

BOBBI: It sure is! It takes a lot of digging...

TWITCHER: We could... We could eat them now...

BOBBI: Good idea... Winter's a long way off... (They gobble up the tulip bulbs greedily.)

Try to consider as an actor:

- That you might have different personalities.
- That you must engage each other in eye contact.
- It is your responsibility to indicate the unseen world around the two characters.
- Creating a line of dramatic involvement which builds up to a memorable climax.
- Working together on supportive physical responses which might include mime sequences.

Brownies

The scene is set in the Brownie Hut, with two girls engaged in some activity appropriate for Brownies. Explore all the mime possibilities.

WENDY: You haven't sewn your new badge on.

NIKKI: Mum didn't have a chance this week...

WENDY: You should sew your own badges on, that's what Brownies are supposed to do, good Brownies...

NIKKI: Don't be a nag, I get enough of that with Mum.

WENDY: Has Brown Owl told you yet about this year's bright idea? You're always late, I bet you missed it...

NIKKI: A pet show, a Brownies pet show... So there! I wasn't late today.

WENDY: It sounds like a good idea.

NIKKI: Yeah! We all have pets, well most of us, that is, except Lucinda Dingle.

WENDY: Well, she's allergic to feathers, fur...

NIKKI: Dust!

WENDY: Milk!

NIKKI: Oranges!

WENDY: Tomatoes!

NIKKI: And her mother!

WENDY: She told me last week when we were making our Valentine cards for our dads, that her mother's feeding her on goats milk an' cheese 'cos she has a permanent rash all over her nose...

NIKKI: I know, it looks awful.

WENDY: Her mum says she's not to go into dusty places...

NIKKI: Do you think that's why she's not here this week?

WENDY: It could be; this hut is the dustiest place you could wish for. It even makes me sneeze…

NIKKI: Yeah! 'Specially when Brown Owl makes us tidy up… Hey, she's looking over… Get a move on…

WENDY: Last week, Lucinda had to go to the porch, gasping for breath an' coughing.

NIKKI: Hasn't she got pills for it?

WENDY: Not that I know of…

NIKKI: Well, she should have. People with allergies take pills all the time…

WENDY: Brown Owl says she's attention seeking, an' puts it all on! I think it's 'cos Lucinda wants Ruth, Liz, Manda and me out there too…because she gets frightened being on her own…

NIKKI: What do you mean?

WENDY: When she has one of her gasping attacks, we all go out to the porch with her. It gets a bit crowded, but we all want to be nurses when we grow up; it's good practice…and we make her do deep breathing exercises…

NIKKI: Why do you do that?

WENDY: We… Well… Manda says… Oh! Don't ask so many questions! What sort of pet are you going to bring to the pet show?

NIKKI: Oh! I'll bring Twitcher…

WENDY: Twitcher?

NIKKI: Yeah! My guinea pig…

WENDY: Well, I'm bringing my Siberian hamster, he's called Putin.

NIKKI: That's a funny name…

WENDY: Dad named him. I call him Chops, 'cos he's always licking his chops!

NIKKI: Brown Owls coming over… We'll never get our badge at this rate…

WENDY: Well, why should you worry, you never sew them on anyway… Yes! Brown Owl we really are concentrating, aren't we Nikki? We're good Brownies…

NIKKI: You bet! (turning and whispering) I can't wait to meet Putin Chops…

WENDY: I just call him Chops...

As actors try to consider:

- That you might have different personalities
- That you must engage each other in eye contact.
- It is your responsibility to indicate the unseen world around the two characters.
- Creating a line of dramatic involvement which builds up to a memorable climax.
- Working together on supportive physical responses which might include mime sequences.

Doing up Bikes

The scene is set in a garage where two boys are doing up a bike: it is a scene full of mime action.

PAUL: Lee!

LEE: All right Paul, I'm over here behind the tea chests. Dad had a mad clean out, and stuck all these tea chests this end, and he said he'll have a Benny if I move 'em.

PAUL: Well, my dad said I can only stay an hour 'cos I'm getting behind in my homework...

LEE: Heck, I haven't done mine in months. You can't do up your BMX an' fit in homework.

PAUL: It's all right for you, you don't go to Monks Park School where teachers do their nut if you don't hand your homework in...

LEE: Oh! Shut up an' hand me that spanner, this cranks too tight and the pedals won't turn.

PAUL: (Handing spanner) Let me look. You've really messed it up since last night. (Having a look.) Oh! You dunce, you've got it round the wrong way...

LEE: You're a fine one to talk, when we were doing up your BMX you put the wheels on back to front and then you spent two hours messing around wondering why they wouldn't fit...

PAUL: All right, all right, you've got a memory like an elephant... (Fiddling with spanner.) There we are, the cranks on the right way around now. Right! Let's have a look at these new wheels you've got...

LEE: (Getting wheels) What do you think?

PAUL: A bit thin, aren't they?

LEE: They're meant to be like that because of the weight.

PAUL: That's all right then. How much did you pay for these?

LEE: £17 each.

PAUL: That's a rip off...

LEE: Not for these type of wheels.

PAUL: OK. Let's see about getting them on. (Mime with machine.)

LEE: Hey, isn't that my phone ringing...

PAUL: Nah! Can't hear a thing...

LEE: It is, hang on, I'll find out what it's about... (Leaves Paul, stands outside garage with iPhone listens and calls out.) It's your dad on the phone, and he says you've got to get home pronto or else you'll be in deep trouble... Do you want to speak to him... (Offering iPhone)

PAUL: Oh! No! He's always nagging, he's worse than Mum. Nah, nah, nah...

LEE: (Waving iPhone) You know he probably heard all that...

PAUL: OK... So I'm in for it...but he did say I could stay for an hour...

As actors try to consider:

- That you might have different personalities.
- That you must engage each other in eye contact.
- It is your responsibility to indicate the unseen world around the two characters.
- Creating a line of dramatic involvement which builds up to a memorable climax.
- Working together on supportive physical responses which might include mime sequences.

Surveying the Castle

Two pupils are visiting a castle; they each have a clipboard with a worksheet to guide them and a plan of the castle. Make up a mime sequence for each moment as the scene is developed.

PICKLE: This whole place is a 'Healthy and Safety' risk.

SAM: It's 'Health and Safety' Pickle, get it right...

PICKLE: And it's going to rain, probably torrential rain... It looks black to me (Looking at the sky). We'll get soaked walking around this place...

SAM: So, you don't like castles?

PICKLE: I didn't say that...did I?

SAM: You've grumbled ever since we walked across that drawbridge...

PICKLE: It's all about 'Health and Safety'. Look at those ramparts (pointing); we could topple off them and go crashing into that old bit of wall...

SAM: Yeah! But Sir has told us not to go climbing up on the ramparts as we are supposed to be studying the castle at ground level. Our investigation is at this level...

PICKLE: That's not much fun...is it? We can't pretend to be medieval knights if we are only kept at ground level...how boring is that!

SAM: Yeah! I suppose you are right, Pickle...what with these clipboards, worksheets and school packed lunches...

PICKLE: I hate school packed lunches...they always give us grated cheese baps...and the cheese falls out all over the place...and there's no pickle to bind it all together...! Like Branston pickle, I do...

SAM: Yeah! Well, we all know that...

PICKLE: And there's always an apple...a green one...why can't it be a banana... I like bananas...

SAM: Will you stop moaning...sketch the motte.

PICKLE: The what?

SAM: The motte.

PICKLE: The moat? There isn't one...

SAM: (Exasperated) That there, Pickle (pointing)...the mound, that big mound.

PICKLE: But there's nothing on it?

SAM: That's because the first Norman castles were made of wood and have disappeared...

PICKLE: Or just burned down by the Anglo-Saxons... I'm on their side... Those Norman knights were killers!

SAM: Those Anglo-Saxon's killed people too...

PICKLE: So, whose side are you on, Sam?

SAM: Look Pickle, we are not here to take sides... But to investigate... Now looking at the plan... We should be standing in the middle of the Knights banqueting hall 'in the centre of the stone castle which replaced the wooden structure in 1098'.

PICKLE: So why didn't they build it on that mound over there?

SAM: I don't know, do I?

PICKLE: But if they had a mound, why didn't they use it?

SAM: It's a man-made mound so perhaps it couldn't support a stone structure...

PICKLE: So why didn't they get rid of the mound?

SAM: (Irritated) Look Pickle! I've never been here before... I'm not a castle specialist... I just want to get through this work sheet...

PICKLE: (Bringing his backpack off his shoulders.) Well, if we are standing in the 'banqueting hall', I think it's time I had my cheese sandwich and apple... (Sitting down)

SAM: You are food obsessed...

PICKLE: So, what! (Getting out his packed lunch.)

SAM: OK. I'll join you. (Bringing his backpack off his shoulders.) School sandwiches, here I come… (He brings them out.)

PICKLE: (Eating) I wonder what medieval Norman knights had for lunch?

SAM: Well, it sure wasn't grated cheese baps with Branston pickle.

PICKLE: Do you think they had imported bananas?

SAM: Pickle! What sort of planet are you on?

PICKLE: I dunno… (Carries on eating his cheese bap.)

As actors try to consider:

- That you might have different personalities
- That you must engage each other in eye contact.
- It is your responsibility to indicate the unseen world around the two characters.
- Creating a line of dramatic involvement which builds up to a memorable climax.
- Working together on supportive physical responses which might include mime sequences.

The School Camp

The scene is set in an established campsite where junior school children come for their weekend with their teachers and friends. The tents they will sleep in have been put up for them. They both have bulging backpacks. During the scene, the contents of these packs can be mimed.

BUZZER: That was a long walk. Why couldn't the bus drive right up?

NIPPY: It's been raining too hard… The lane was full of deep ruts and Sir didn't want to take any risks.

BUZZER: Miss said if we got stuck, we could all push…

NIPPY: I wouldn't want to push the school minibus…

BUZZER: With Sir and Miss and the twelve of us, it would be OK…

NIPPY: Well, I'm glad we got out and walked up here.

(They sit down and open their backpacks.)

BUZZER: I could do with a drink (drinks from bottle).

NIPPY: (Look at label) Oh! No! Mum's given me still water. She knows I like lemon and lime, not just water!

BUZZER: Nippy! Water is better for you, with, like, no additives…

NIPPY: But I like additives like lemon and lime.

BUZZER: My bottled water says (reads) bottled from 'spring water high in the Brecon Beacons' and that's where we are. Just breathe in the fresh air Nippy…

NIPPY: This place seems damp to me. And where are the shops? (looks around) There isn't a single shop anywhere…

BUZZER: It's because this is an eco-centre… (Stretches arms and looks up to the sky.) Just enjoy the sunshine and peace and quiet.

NIPPY: (Rummaging in his backpack.) That sun is really bright...! Hope Mum has put in my sunscreen (Brings out bottle). Oh! No! It's 'factor 15' what is she on; she knows I need factor 50 or I burn up! (Standing up)

BUZZER: Just put on two layers...

NIPPY: That would only make it 30... (Rubbing some on)

BUZZER: (Fed up) Then put a third one on, build up the protection...

NIPPY: But that's only factor 45...

BUZZER: Do you know you haven't stopped moaning since we got here. Sir said we are here to enjoy the 'Ecology'; can't you just relax. Look! (waving his arms around) enjoy all the ecology like me. You've got your sunscreen on so just sit down Nippy...

(Nippy sits down alongside Buzzer, but is not very happy.)

NIPPY: (Jumping up) A snake! (Pointing) I saw a snake in the grass there...

BUZZER: Just calm down! There aren't any venomous snakes in the UK...

NIPPY: Are you sure?

BUZZER: Yeah! That's what my dad says when we go camping...

NIPPY: But is he right? (Getting out iPhone and using it.) I'm going to check that...

BUZZER: My dad's always right...

NIPPY: No, he isn't! It says here: 'The adder or viper is the only venomous reptile in the UK'.

BUZZER: (Taking iPhone and reading.) OK! 'So adder or viper'. Dad must have meant Ireland 'cos I remember now he said something about St Patrick ridding Ireland of snakes...

NIPPY: And it says 'venomous' (Takes back iPhone)

BUZZER: That doesn't mean its venom will kill you...

NIPPY: Buzzer do you always look on the bright side?

BUZZER: Yeah! 'Cos it says: 'It's generally shy and non-aggressive...'

NIPPY: Well, I'm going to look inside our tent...

(Nippy goes to peer inside the tent to see what it is like.)
BUZZER: (Going towards him.) What's it like in there?
NIPPY: Smells damp.
BUZZER: Well, this is Wales...
NIPPY: Oh no! There's a spider, a big spider (Stiffens and grimace). I am definitely not sleeping in there...
BUZZER: Yeah! It could be a tarantula brought in on a banana...
NIPPY: Stop! You're winding me up Buzzer...
BUZZER: (Going to peer inside the tent.) It's the smallest, tiniest, piddling little spider I've ever seen... Stop being a big baby...
NIPPY: (Waving arms) Miss! Miss! There's a big spider in my tent...come and get it out please...
BUZZER: (Watching the reaction from Miss.) Well, Nippy, by the way, she's running off in the opposite direction I would guess Miss doesn't like spiders either...
NIPPY: (Agitated) But she's supposed to be looking after us... Miss! Miss! Come back... Please...

As actors try to consider:

- That you might have different personalities
- That you must engage each other in eye contact.
- It is your responsibility to indicate the unseen world around the two characters.
- Creating a line of dramatic involvement which builds up to a memorable climax.
- Working together on supportive physical responses which might include mime sequences.